Contents

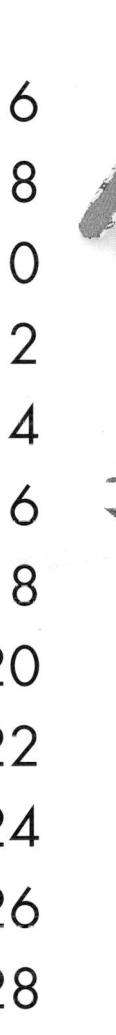

Be cool. Tidy our school.

Home sweet home

Do you live in a town, by the sea or out in the countryside? Wherever you live, there are different habitats for you to see. These include fields, roads, woods, hedgerows, wastelands, parks, gardens, building sites, rivers and streams, or the seashore.

Hedgerows are a perfect habitat for many insects, birds and small animals.

A habitat is a special place where certain groups of animals and plants live. It might be large, like an ocean, a rainforest, a desert, or the icy places around the Poles. Or it could be small — a pond, a wood, or a wasteland area in a town.

Each habitat will give its plants and animals food, air, water and a place to live. Some animals and insects are so small that we need to use a magnifying glass to see them. But just because they are small does not mean they are not important.

You may need to look hard to see some creatures.

✂ HAVE A GO!

Go out with an adult and explore the area around you. How many different habitats can you find? Compare the creatures and plants that you found in the different places.

✱ WATCH OUT!

Always go with an adult you know when you are out and about. Remember to take great care by water or at the seaside.

A chain reaction

We share the world with an amazing number of plants and animals which all live in many different habitats.

This flower provides food for this butterfly.

Animals and plants depend on each other for food, which they find in their habitats. An owl may eat a mouse, which in turn, eats seeds and berries. This is called a 'food chain'.

HAVE A GO!

Make a food chain mobile. Cut out pictures of plants, birds and small mammals from magazines. Hang them in the correct order, like in this picture.

Can you think of longer food chains?

Habitats don't stay the same for ever, they change slowly over time. They are linked to each other. If one is damaged or destroyed it affects those around it.

HAVE A GO!

Set up a line of dominoes on end. Gently tap the first domino and watch what happens. Habitats are like this – if we change something in one habitat, it affects another one too.

We must get rid of our waste carefully, otherwise it pollutes the countryside.

People, like animals, rely on the environment for a place to live. But people can damage habitats if they are not careful. We need to protect habitats, otherwise we will upset the balance of nature.

A lot of litter

It's fun to be able to explore different areas – perhaps going for a walk in the countryside, or visiting different towns. But it's easy to think that it doesn't matter if we drop just one crisp packet or drink can, thinking someone else will pick it up.

Litter is rubbish that is in the wrong place. It is a big problem in towns and the countryside. It pollutes streams, is a danger to wildlife and makes places look horrible.

Places that are clean and free from litter are a pleasure to look at and visit.

Plastic bags can be eaten by animals or can get stuck over their heads. Sharp objects cut feet and paws. Mice and voles can get trapped inside bottles – unable to get food, they starve.

10

✂ HAVE A GO!

Some rubbish rots down easily. Other things do not. Find out what rots by burying things like an apple-core, a tin can, a piece of cardboard, a plastic crisp bag and a glass bottle. Don't forget to label the places well. You will have to be patient and wait about 6 to 8 weeks before you dig them up again. What did you find?

Waste that rots down, such as vegetable and plant waste, can be put onto a compost heap. Compost is put onto the soil and helps plants to grow.

Rubbish that does not rot down can be sorted through to see what can be re-used or recycled. Rubbish that cannot be re-used or recycled needs to be thrown away carefully.

Farming the countryside

Farmers have the important job of growing the food we all eat. Their work of ploughing, growing crops and harvesting changes how the countryside looks all year round.

A lot of the work farmers do keeps the countryside in good condition. But some of their work can also harm wildlife. Farmers often use pesticides to kill insects that eat their crops. They use fertilisers to make their crops grow. These can harm other plants and animals that they are not meant for.

Some pesticides can stay on plants and insects and get eaten by birds and other wildlife. If the chemicals stay in their bodies, they can build up and cause harm.

Fertilisers and pesticides need to be used carefully.

FASCINATING FACT!

DDT was a pesticide that was used in many countries. It was found in the bodies of penguins at the South Pole, where the pesticide hadn't been used at all. How do you think it got there?

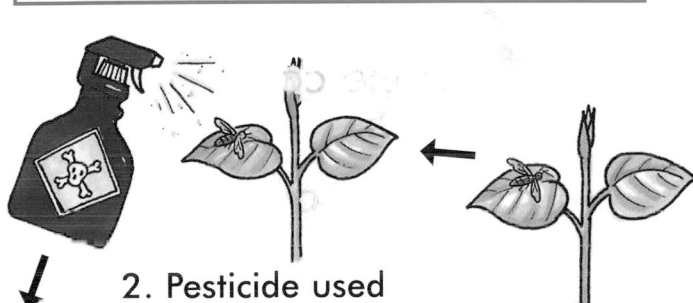

2. Pesticide used to kill insect pest

1. Pest eats crop

3. Bird eats sprayed insect

4. Spray on insect poisons bird

5. Fox eats poisoned bird

LOOK BACK

Look back to page 8 find out about food chains.

Helpful habitats

Different habitats are important for different reasons. Trees help to give us fresh air. When trees make their food, they use up some of a gas called carbon dioxide (the gas we breathe out). This helps to keep the air clean and stops the earth from heating up too much. Trees give out oxygen (the gas we breathe in).

If trees are cut down, they can no longer help to control the temperature of the earth.

Trees not only help clean the air, they also provide homes for insects, birds and animals.

Trees are also important for holding soil together. Tree roots grow a long way below the ground. If trees are cut down, their roots disappear, then there is nothing to keep the soil together. It can get washed away in rainstorms (right). This is how some deserts have been made.

✂ HAVE A GO!

Plant some cress in loose compost on a large, flat tray. When it is grown, split the compost in half. You can see how the roots hold on to the soil and keep it together. This is how the roots of trees work as well.

Wet areas, like marshes, ponds and lakes, are important habitats too. Draining ponds and marshes for new fields or for building houses and roads can leave animals and insects who depend on these habitats with nowhere to live.

Be a litter picker!

Did you have crisps or a chocolate bar to eat today? What did you do with the bag or wrapper? Not everyone puts their rubbish in the bin.

✂ HAVE A GO!

Are their areas in your school where litter collects? Do you think your litter-bins are in the right places? Could they be moved to better places?

Organise a litter pick around school with your classmates. Don't forget to wear gloves or wash your hands carefully afterwards. Design a colourful poster telling people to put their rubbish in the bin.

Be cool. Tidy our school.

👀 LOOK BACK

Look back to page 10 to find out about litter spoiling places.

16

How often have you seen takeaway food packaging, crisp packets and drink cans just lying around?

Many of these things could have been recycled if they had been put in the right place.

If you do a litter pick, see what sort of rubbish you find the most of.

FASCINATING FACT!

In the City of Westminster, a part of London, about 50 tonnes of litter are collected off the streets every day.

Every year, we throw away about 1 million tonnes of litter.

Follow the Country Code

The countryside is an important place for animals to make their homes and for plants to grow. Careless actions can spoil wild places forever. But if we follow a few simple rules, we can help to protect the countryside. Remember to follow the Country Code.

The Country Code

Follow these simple rules and be a good country guest.

- ❁ Close gates. Keep your dog under control.
- ❁ Take care not to start fires.
- ❁ Take litter home with you.
- ❁ Don't pollute water.
- ❁ Keep to paths.
- ❁ Don't damage walls and fences.
- ❁ Leave farm animals alone.
- ❁ Don't make unnecessary noise.

HAVE A GO!

Get together with some friends to make up your own 'Country Code' board game. Use clues like 'close gates' 'keep your dog under control' to take you forwards on the board, and 'drop litter' or 'pick wild flowers' to take you backwards.

START

PICK WILD FLOWERS BACK 3 SPACES

8

CONTROL YOUR DOG FORWARD 2 SPACES

1
2
6
5
4
10
11
12

CLOSE GATE FORWARD 2 SPACES

DROP LITTER BACK 3 SPACES

FINISH

14
15

It is possible to buy many different types of flowers to cheer up your home, like these. Don't pick wild flowers though.

FASCINATING FACT!

It is illegal to dig up wild flowers from the countryside. If you want them in your garden, buy them from a specialist wildflower nursery. Your local Wildlife Trust will help you.

Go organic

Some farmers and gardeners are concerned that too many pesticides and fertilisers are used to grow food. These people use organic methods to grow their crops and plants. This means trying to use more natural ways to fertilise flowers, fruits and vegetables.

Look in your local fruit and vegetable shops to see if they sell organically-grown goods.

Animal manure, a natural fertiliser, is sometimes used instead of chemicals.

Crops are grown in different fields each year so the soil doesn't get too tired by growing the same crop.

FASCINATING FACT!

Nature has its own natural pest-control. Hedgehogs eat slugs, which can damage crops. Ladybirds eat greenfly – another pest that often attacks plants. In California, in the USA, farmers buy ladybird grubs to put onto their crops to help to keep them pest-free.

HAVE A GO!

You can grow your own organic vegetables at home or school. If you do not have much space, buy mini-vegetable seeds and plant them in a window box or grow-bag. Remove any pests by hand (wear gloves) and use only natural fertilisers.

21

Helping the habitats

There used to be many more trees in Britain and across the world, but as more and more people need somewhere to live or grow their crops, more forests are cleared.

👀 **LOOK BACK**

Look back to pages 14 and 15 to see how important trees are.

But we can help protect woodlands and wetland.

When you buy greetings cards, choose ones that are made from recycled paper, or paper made from 'sustainable forests'. These are forests where trees are planted to replace the ones cut down.

If your family buys new wooden furniture, ask them to buy woods that are grown in sustainable forests, especially those that grow quickly so do not take long to replace.

✂ HAVE A GO!

Paper and cardboard are made from wood. We can all help reduce the amount of trees cut down to make paper by re-using envelopes, recycling paper and by buying recycled paper goods.

❋ WATCH OUT!

If you have a pond in your nature reserve, make sure you only go near it when you are with an adult.

We can help protect wet areas too. Think carefully about how you use water. If it does not rain for a while, save water by using the washing-up water to give the garden a drink. This will leave more water in lakes and reservoirs. What other ways can you think of that will help to save water?

Have you got a nature reserve area at school? If not, is there room to start one?

Be a good guest

Everyone loves a holiday, whether you stay at home or go abroad. But tourists can do a lot of damage to the places they go to visit: noise frightens animals, extra sewage may be pumped into the sea, and lots of people walking along the same path may wear it away.

✂ HAVE A GO!

Write a 'Good Tourist Guide' telling people how to take care of the places they visit. Include suggestions in it about the Country Code, noise, pollution, picking up litter and remembering to be a good 'guest' wherever you are.

Some problems seem so big that it may seem there is nothing that we can do to help. But there is.

Remember the Country Code when you are out and about. You don't just have to be in the country for it to be important.

There are other things that you can do to help as well:

- ❁ Enjoy the countryside (left), but leave it how you would like to find it.

- ❁ Think carefully about how you use water.

- ❁ Re-use and recycle as many things as you can.

- ❁ Buy organically grown fruit and vegetables. Or even better, grow your own.

By thinking carefully about how we behave when we are visiting other places, or even when we are in the places where we live, we can help to protect nature.

More activities and facts

 **FASCINATING FACT!**

The world's tropical rainforests are home to over five million species of animals, plants and insects.

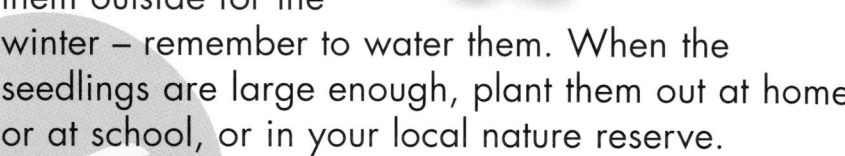 **HAVE A GO!**

Collect some tree seeds such as acorns, conkers or sycamore 'helicopters'. Plant them in pots and leave them outside for the winter – remember to water them. When the seedlings are large enough, plant them out at home or at school, or in your local nature reserve.

Always check first, though, that you are planting a tree where a tree belongs.

 **HAVE A GO!**

Find out about organisations such as WWF, Greenpeace and Friends of the Earth. They all work to protect wildlife and save the oceans from pollution such as sewage, nuclear-waste and chemical dumping, and oil-spills.

 **FASCINATING FACT!**

Trees put water back into the air through their leaves.

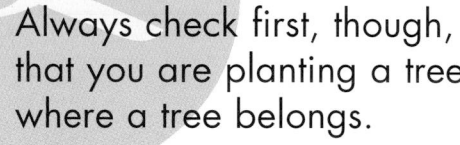

✂ HAVE A GO!

Find pictures of different habitats in books or on a CD-ROM. Compare them with the habitats in your local area. Look at the different plants and animals in them.

👀 LOOK BACK

Look back to pages 18 and 19 to remind yourself about the Country Code.

! FASCINATING FACT!

All of the countryside in Britain belongs to somcone. Some land is private and is owned by people like farmers. The law says that you are not allowed to go across this land unless you have the landowner's permission.
You may go across land where there is a public footpath or bridleway.

Some areas of our countryside are owned by the government. These include National Parks. National Parks are protected areas.

✂ HAVE A GO!

A garden at home or school can become a wildlife reserve all of its own. Plant scented bushes and flowers for butterflies and bees. A pond will be home to frogs, toads and other water-creatures. Hedgehogs like a pile of leaves or old logs.

Useful words

carbon dioxide: a gas that is in the air.

chemicals: chemicals can be found in pesticides and fertilisers. They help pesticides kill insects that eat crops. The chemicals in fertilisers help crops to grow.

desert: an area that is often sandy and where few plants grow.

environment: the air, land and water where plants, people and animals live.

extinct: when a plant or animal species dies out completely.

harvesting: the gathering in of crops and food.

ocean: a very large sea.

organic food: food produced without using chemical pesticides or fertilisers.

poles: the areas around the North and South Poles.

pollute: to make the land, air or water dirty.

rainforest: a dense forest that has heavy rainfall.

species: a group of animals or plants which are of the same type and which will breed together.

tropical: an area that has a hot climate.

recycle: to make something new out of something which has been used before.

wildlife reserve: a protected area set aside for wildlife to live in.

reservoir: a lake used for storing water.

sewage: water which contains waste products flushed down drains, sinks and toilets.

Index